*"Laughter is the
closest distance
between two
people."*

— VICTOR BORGE

Super Funny
Knock! Knock! Jokes
and More!

FOR KIDS

Super Funny Knock-Knock Jokes and More for Kids is an original work, first published in 2021 by Fox Chapel Publishing Company, Inc. Reproduction of its contents is strictly prohibited without written permission from the rights holder.

ISBN 978-1-64124-142-7

Library of Congress Control Number: 2021943154

To learn more about the other great books from Fox Chapel Publishing, or to find a retailer near you, call toll-free 800-457-9112 or visit us at *www.FoxChapelPublishing.com*.

We are always looking for talented authors. To submit an idea, please send a brief inquiry to acquisitions@foxchapelpublishing.com.

Fox Chapel Publishing makes every effort to use environmentally friendly paper for printing.

Printed in the United States of America
First printing

Knock Knock Jokes Through History

Knock knock jokes have been around a long time. How long? Well, it's hard to say. But we'd guess that knock knock jokes almost certainly appeared sometime after the invention of the first door and possibly before the first doorbell. So much for the history lesson.

The important thing is this: Some knock knock jokes make people **laugh** while other knock knock jokes make people **groan**. We've filled this book with both kinds, so you'll have to try them all out on your friends and family to see which are which.

What's cool is that you can tell knock knock jokes almost anywhere. You don't even need a real door! You just say "knock knock" and people will instantly ask, "Who's there?" That doesn't always happen when you actually knock on a real door. Amazing!

In addition to lots of knock knock jokes, this book contains an assortment of regular jokes, too. You could say "knock knock" before telling these jokes, but that would be kind of silly. And this book is silly enough as it is! **Enjoy!**

Knock! Knock!

Who's there?

Etch.

Etch who?

Eww! You sneezed on your door!

Knock! Knock!

Who's there?

Leaf.

Leaf who?

Leaf me alone, please!

Knock! Knock!
Who's there?
Mustache.
Mustache who?
I mustache you a question, but I'll shave it for later.

Knock! Knock!
Who's there?
Ketchup.
Ketchup who?
**Ketchup with me,
I'm pretty fast!**

Knock! Knock!

Who's there?

Alex.

Alex who?

Alex the questions around here!

Knock! Knock!

Who's there?

Luke.

Luke who?

Luke out the window to find out!

Knock! Knock!

Who's there?

Cannelloni.

Cannelloni who?

Cannelloni a few bucks until I get my allowance?

Knock! Knock!

Who's there?

Bacon.

Bacon who?

Bacon some cookies in there?

Knock! Knock!
Who's there?
Honeybee.
Honeybee who?
Honeybee a dear and open the door.

Knock! Knock!
Who's there?
Chickens.
Chickens who?
No, no. Chickens cluck. Owls whoo!

Knock! Knock!
Who's there?
Wood.
Wood who?
Wood you just open the door?

Knock! Knock!
Who's there?
Iran.
Iran who?
Iran here from far away.

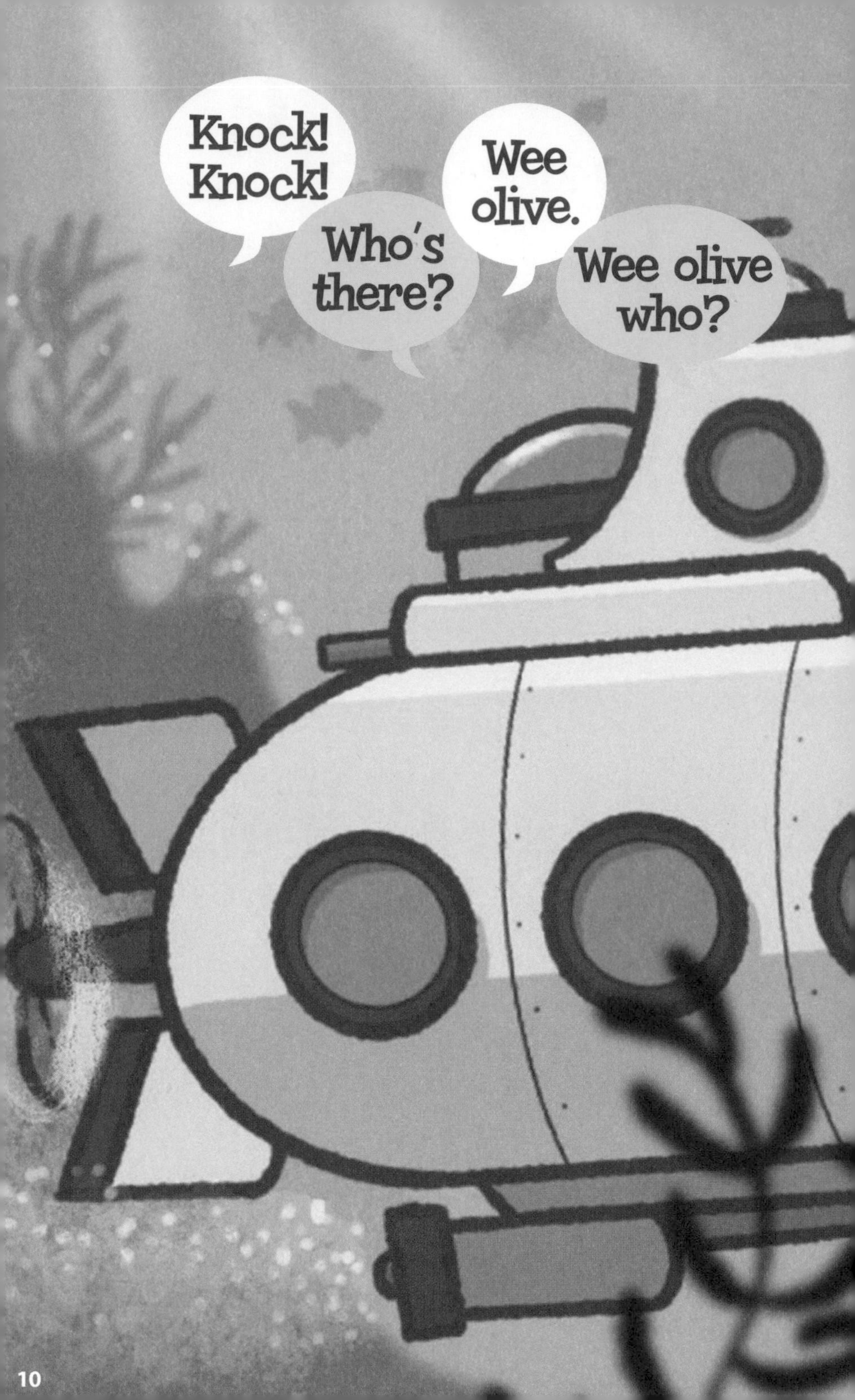
Knock! Knock!
Who's there?
Wee olive.
Wee olive who?

Knock! Knock!

Who's there?

Nana.

Nana who?

Nana your business!

Knock! Knock!

Who's there?

Turnip.

Turnip who?

Turnip your doorbell so you can hear it.

Knock! Knock!

Who's there?

Abby

Abby who?

Abby birthday to you!

12

Knock! Knock!
Who's there?
Eggs.
Eggs who?
Eggstremely surprised you don't know who it is!

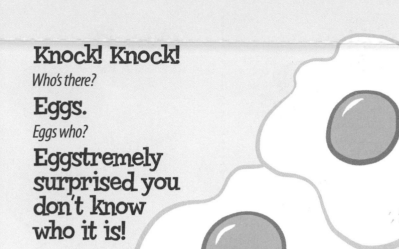

Knock! Knock!

Who's there?

Summer.

Summer who?

Summer here and summer there.

Knock! Knock!

Who's there?

Ben.

Ben who?

Ben knocking for quite a while!

Knock! Knock!

Who's there?

Says.

Says who?

Says ME, that's who!

Knock! Knock!

Who's there?

Tank.

Tank who?

You're welcome.

Knock! Knock!
Who's there?
Purple alligator.
Purple alligator who?
Wait. Just how many purple alligators do you know?

Knock! Knock!
Who's there?

Ghosts.
Ghosts who?

Ghosts stand away from the door so I can come in!

Knock! Knock!

Who's there?

Canoe.

Canoe who?

Canoe just open the door?

Knock! Knock!

Who's there?

Adore.

Adore who?

Adore is between us. Open up!

Knock! Knock!

Who's there?

Emma.

Emma who?

Emma bit cold out here! Let me in!

Knock! Knock!

Who's there?

Snow.

Snow who?

Snow one's at the door!

Knock! Knock!

Who's there?

Ice cream.

Ice cream who?

Ice cream as loud as I can, but no one answers the door!

Knock! Knock!

Who's there?

Harry

Harry who?

Harry up and open the door! It's freezing out here!

Knock! Knock!

Who's there?

Ida.

Ida who?

No, not Ida-who. It's pronounced Idaho!

Knock! Knock!

Who's there?

Annie.

Annie who?

Annie thing you can do, I can do better!

Knock! Knock!

Who's there?

Taco.

Taco who?

Taco 'bout it after you open your door!

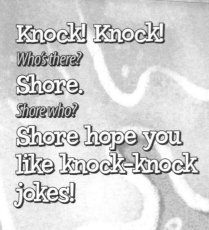

Knock! Knock!
Who's there?
Shore.
Shore who?
Shore hope you like knock-knock jokes!

Knock! Knock!
Who's there?
Roach.
Roach who?
Roach you a note saying I was coming over!

Knock! Knock!
Who's there?
Lion.
Lion who?
Lion all the time. No one believes me!

What did one toilet say
to the other?

What did the Dalmatian say
after dinner?

Why are there so few birthday
parties on Mars?

What's black and white
and red all over?

What do you call an alligator
in a vest?

It takes too long
to planet.

An embarrassed
penguin.

An investigator!

"That meal really hit
the spot!"

"You look a little flushed."

Knock! Knock!
Who's there?
Ants.
Ants who?
Knock! Knock!
Who's there?
Ants.
Ants who?
Knock! Knock!
Who's there?
Ants.
Ants who?
Knock! Knock!
Who's there?
Ants.
Ants who?
Knock! Knock!
Who's there?
Uncle.
Uncle who?
Uncle who is glad you got rid of all those ants!

Knock! Knock!
Who's there?
Sarah.
Sarah who?
Sarah phone I can use? My car's out of gas!

Knock! Knock!

Who's there?

Zaire.

Zaire who?

Zaire anyone home today?

Knock! Knock!

Who's there?

Watts.

Watts who?

Watts for dinner tonight?

Knock! Knock!

Who's there?

Goat.

Goat who?

Goat to the door and you'll find out!

Knock! Knock!

Who's there?

Wanda.

Wanda who?

Wanda stop by and visit!

Knock! Knock!

Who's there?

Amos.

Amos who?

Amos-quito just bit me!

Knock! Knock!
Who's there?
Carl.
Carl who?
Carl get you there faster than walking.

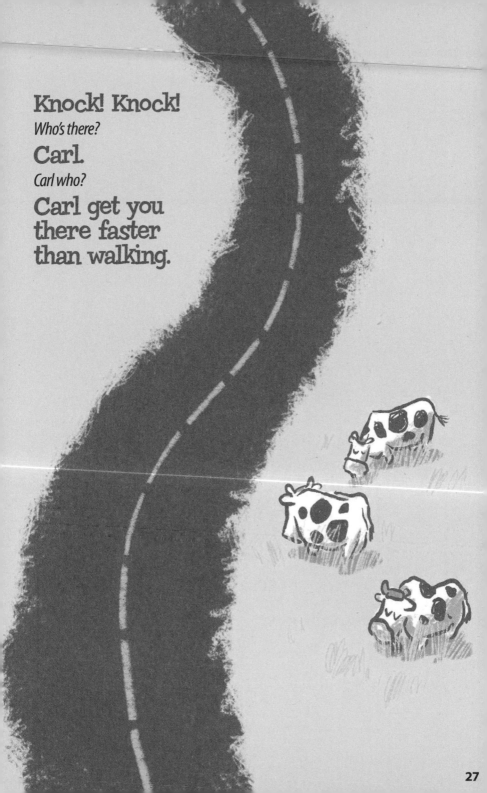

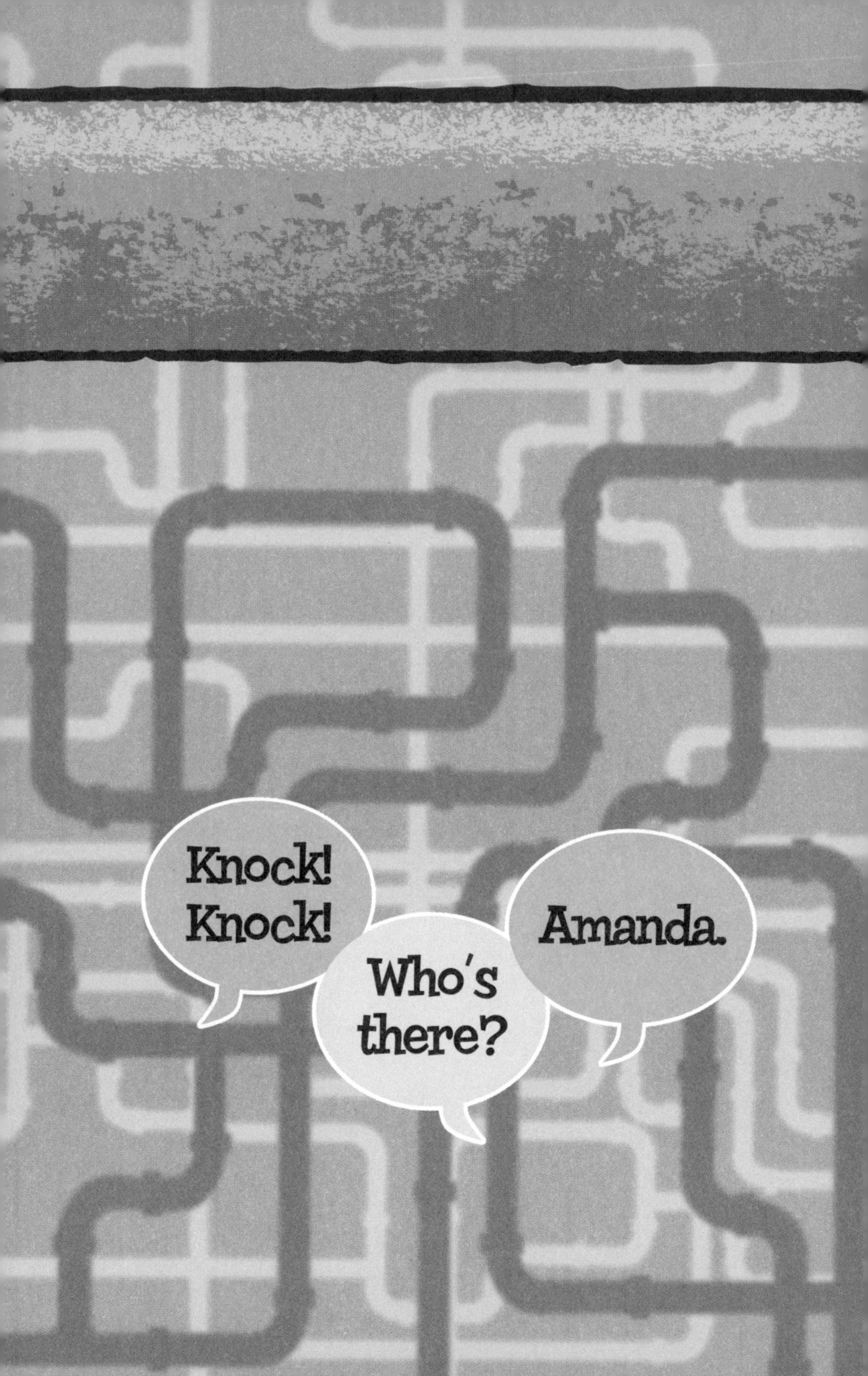
Knock! Knock!
Who's there?
Amanda.

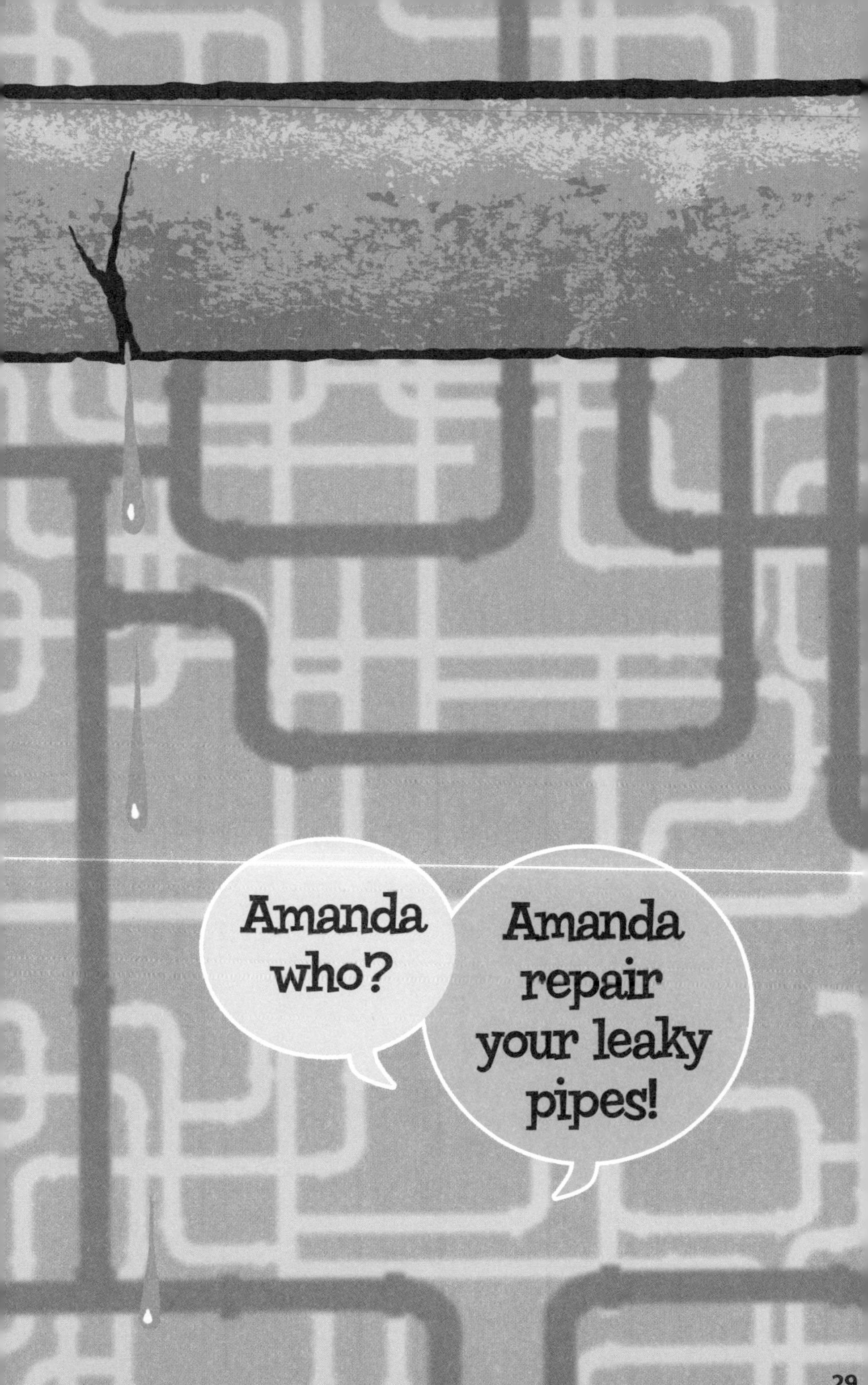
Amanda who?
Amanda repair your leaky pipes!

Knock! Knock!

Who's there?

Althea.

Althea who?

Althea later. I gotta go now!

Knock! Knock!

Who's there?

Hans.

Hans who?

Hans off my candy bar!

Knock! Knock!

Who's there?

Butter

Butter who?

Butter open the door now if you want to find out!

Knock! Knock!
Who's there?
Banana.
Banana who?
Knock! Knock!
Who's there?
Banana.
Banana who?
Knock! Knock!
Who's there?
Banana.
Banana who?
Knock! Knock!
Who's there?
Banana.
Banana who?
Knock! Knock!
Who's there?
Lemon.
Lemon who?
Lemon know if you want another bunch of bananas!

Knock! Knock!

Who's there?

Esther.

Esther who?

Esther anybody home?

Knock! Knock!

Who's there?

Norma Lee.

Norma Lee who?

Norma Lee I just ring the bell.

Knock! Knock!
Who's there?
Stopwatch.
Stopwatch who?
Stopwatch you're doing and open the door!

Knock! Knock!

Who's there?

Four eggs.

Four eggs who?

Four eggs ample, I made breakfast!

Knock! Knock!

Who's there?

Candice.

Candice who?

Candice be the right address?

Knock! Knock!
Who's there?
Pudding.
Pudding who?
Pudding my shoes on. I'll be right there!

37

Knock! Knock!

Who's there?

Fur.

Fur who?

Furgot to tell you I was coming over!

Knock! Knock!

Who's there?

Sacha.

Sacha who?

Sacha lot of questions you ask!

Knock! Knock!

Who's there?

Sadie.

Sadie who?

Sadie magic word and I'll share my cookies.

Knock! Knock!

Who's there?

Iona.

Iona who?

Iona lot of toy animals.

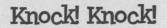

What is fast, loud
and crispy?

How do you know when Dracula
isn't feeling well?

Why couldn't the pony
sing with the choir?

What did one kitchen wall
say to the other?

What did the magician say
to the fisherman?

She was a little horse.

"Let's meet at the corner for lunch."

"Pick a cod, any cod."

A rocket chip!

You hear a lot of coffin.

Jumbled Jokes

These clowns need your help! Can you match each joke with the correct punchline?

A: Swimming trunks.

Q: What do you get when you mix cows and a trampoline?

Q: What do you get when you mix a cheetah and a hamburger?

Q: What do you get when you mix a cat and a bird?

Q: What do you get when you mix a turtle and a porcupine?

A: The wurst headache.

A: Dollars and scents!

A:
Fast food!

Q: What do you get when you mix a hot dog and really loud music?

A:
Shredded tweet!

Q: What do you get when you mix a fish and an elephant?

A:
A slowpoke!

A:
Milkshakes!

Q: What do you get when you mix a bank and a skunk?

43

Knock! Knock!

Who's there?

Ada.

Ada who?

Ada bowl of cereal this morning.

Knock! Knock!

Who's there?

Hammond.

Hammond who?

Hammond eggs!

Knock! Knock!
Who's there?
Cook.
Cook who?
You sound like a cuckoo clock!

Knock! Knock!
Who's there?
Bed.
Bed who?
Bed you'll never guess who this is!

Knock! Knock!

Who's there?

Troy.

Troy who?

Troy to answer the door faster, please!

Knock! Knock!

Who's there?

Value.

Value who?

Value ever open this door?

45

Knock! Knock!

Who's there?

Yeah.

Yeah who?

Take it easy! Don't get so excited!

Knock! Knock!

Who's there?

Nobel

Nobel who?

Nobel, so I knocked instead!

Knock! Knock!
Who's there?
Heaven.
Heaven who?
Heaven seen you for such a long time!

46

Knock! Knock!
Who's there?
Boo.
Boo who?
Hey now, there's no need to cry about it!

Knock! Knock!

Who's there?

Roman

Roman who?

Roman around knocking on doors.

Knock! Knock!

Who's there?

Sherwood.

Sherwood who?

Sherwood be grateful if you let me in!

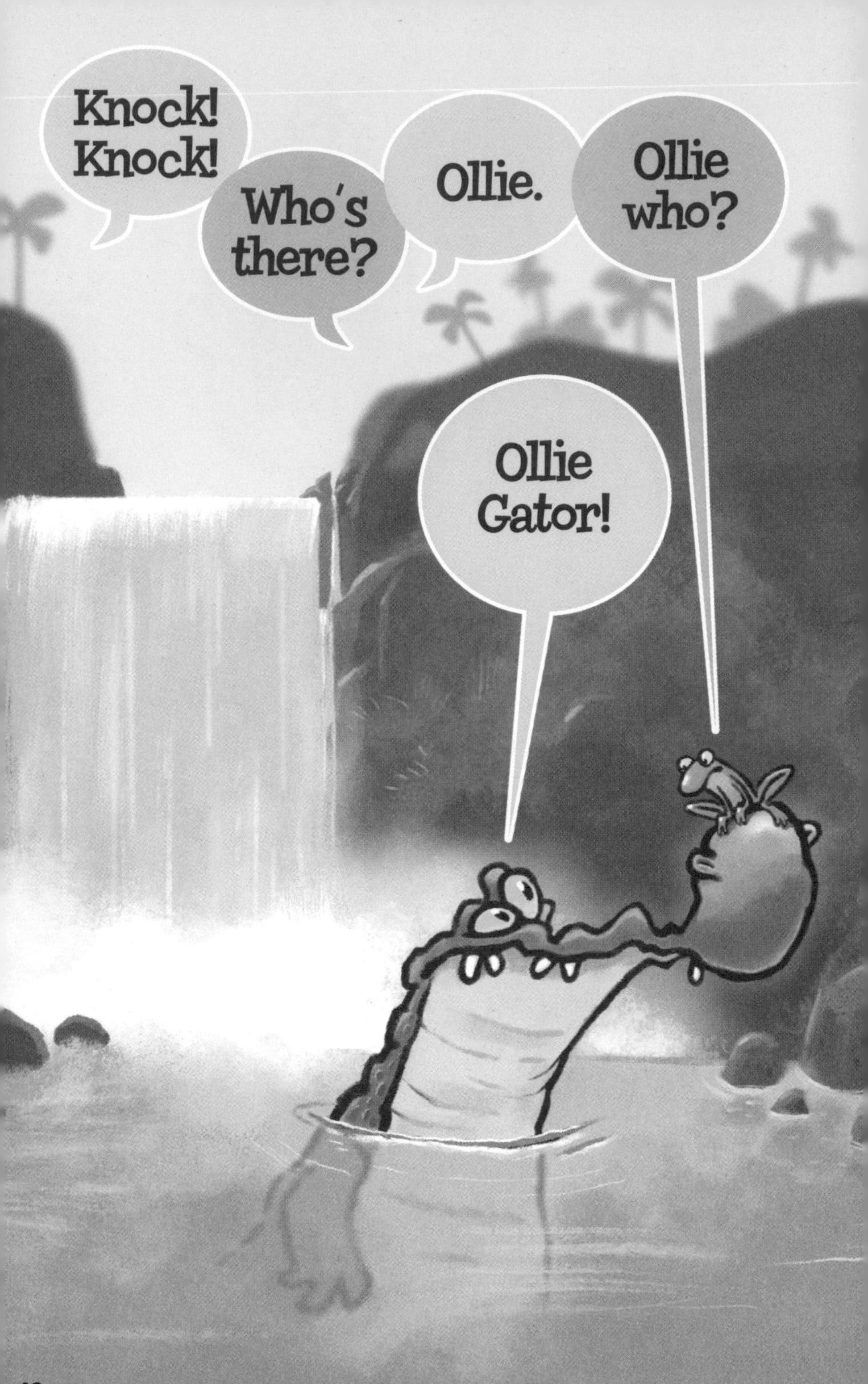
Knock! Knock!
Who's there?
Ollie.
Ollie who?
Ollie Gator!

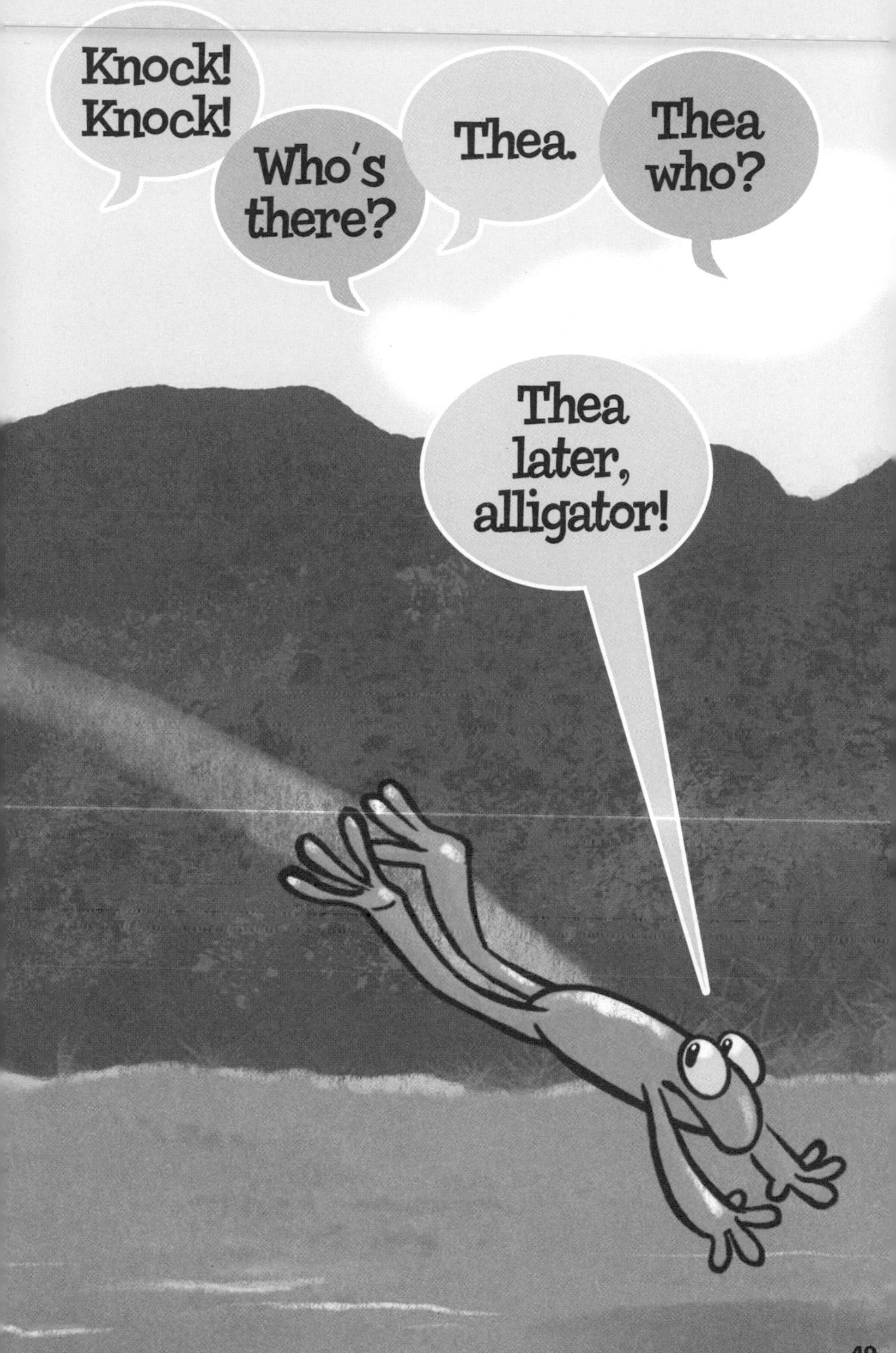

Knock! Knock!
Who's there?
Thea.
Thea who?
Thea later, alligator!

Knock! Knock!

Who's there?

Dishes.

Dishes who?

Dishes your best friend!

Knock! Knock!

Who's there?

Russian.

Russian who?

Russian to get inside! Open up!

Knock! Knock!
Who's there?
Teresa
Teresa who?
Teresa green in the summertime!

Knock! Knock!
Who's there?
Rita.
Rita who?
Rita lot of books every month.

Knock! Knock!

Who's there?

Alfie.

Alfie who?

Alfie just awful if you leave!

Knock! Knock!

Who's there?

Voodoo.

Voodoo who?

Voodoo you think it is?

Knock! Knock!

Who's there?

Lefty.

Lefty who?

Lefty key at home so I had to knock!

Knock! Knock!

Who's there?

CD.

CD. who?

CD text I sent you yesterday?

Knock! Knock!
Who's there?
West.
West who?
West awhile after soccer practice.

Knock! Knock!
Who's there?
Detail.
Detail who?
Detail of a tiger should never, ever be pulled!

Knock! Knock!

Who's there?

Halibut.

Halibut who?

Halibut we go to the movies this weekend?

Knock! Knock!

Who's there?

Wood ant.

Wood ant who?

Wood ant you like some fresh popcorn?

Knock! Knock! *Who's there?* **Orange.** *Orange who?* **Knock! Knock!** *Who's there?* **Orange.** *Orange who?*

Knock! Knock!

Who's there?

Venice.

Venice who?

Venice dinner going to be ready?

Knock! Knock!

Who's there?

Isabel.

Isabel who?

Isabel working? I had to knock.

Knock! Knock!
Who's there?
Broken pencil.
Broken pencil who?
Nevermind. There's no point.

56

Knock! Knock!
Who's there?
Cash.
Cash who?
No, thanks. But I'll take some peanuts if you have any.

Knock! Knock!
Who's there?
Hawaii.
Hawaii who?
I'm fine. Hawaii you?

Knock! Knock!
Who's there?
Anita.
Anita who?
Anita borrow a few bucks!

Knock! Knock!

Who's there?

Justin.

Justin who?

Justin time! I was about to leave!

Knock! Knock!

Who's there?

Alaska.

Alaska who?

Alaska gain. Can you open up?

Knock! Knock!
Who's there?
Alpaca.
Alpaca who?
Alpaca suitcase, you fill up the car.

Knock! Knock!
Who's there?
A herd.
A herd who?
A herd you were back in town and I wanted to pay a visit.

Knock! Knock!

Who's there?

Comb.

Comb who?

Comb open the door, you'll see.

Knock! Knock!

Who's there?

Spell.

Spell who?

W-H-O. Now can I come in?

Knock! Knock!

Who's there?

Utah.

Utah who?

Utah king to me?

Knock! Knock!

Who's there?

Jess.

Jess who?

Jess me and a few of my friends!

Knock! Knock!
Who's there?
Ears.
Ears who?
Ears looking at you, kid!

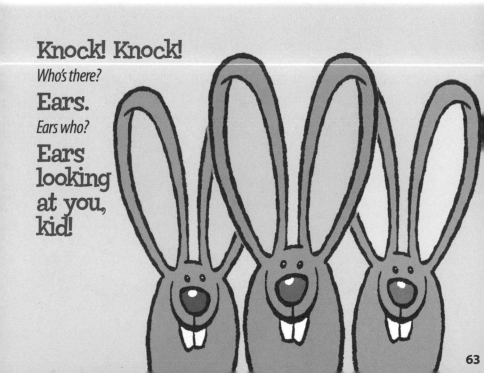

63

Knock! Knock!

Who's there?

Luke.

Luke who?

Luke through the peephole!

Knock! Knock!

Who's there?

Beef.

Beef who?

Beef-ore I freeze, can you open up?

Knock! Knock!
Who's there?
Who Who.
Who Who who?
Santa Claus, is that you?

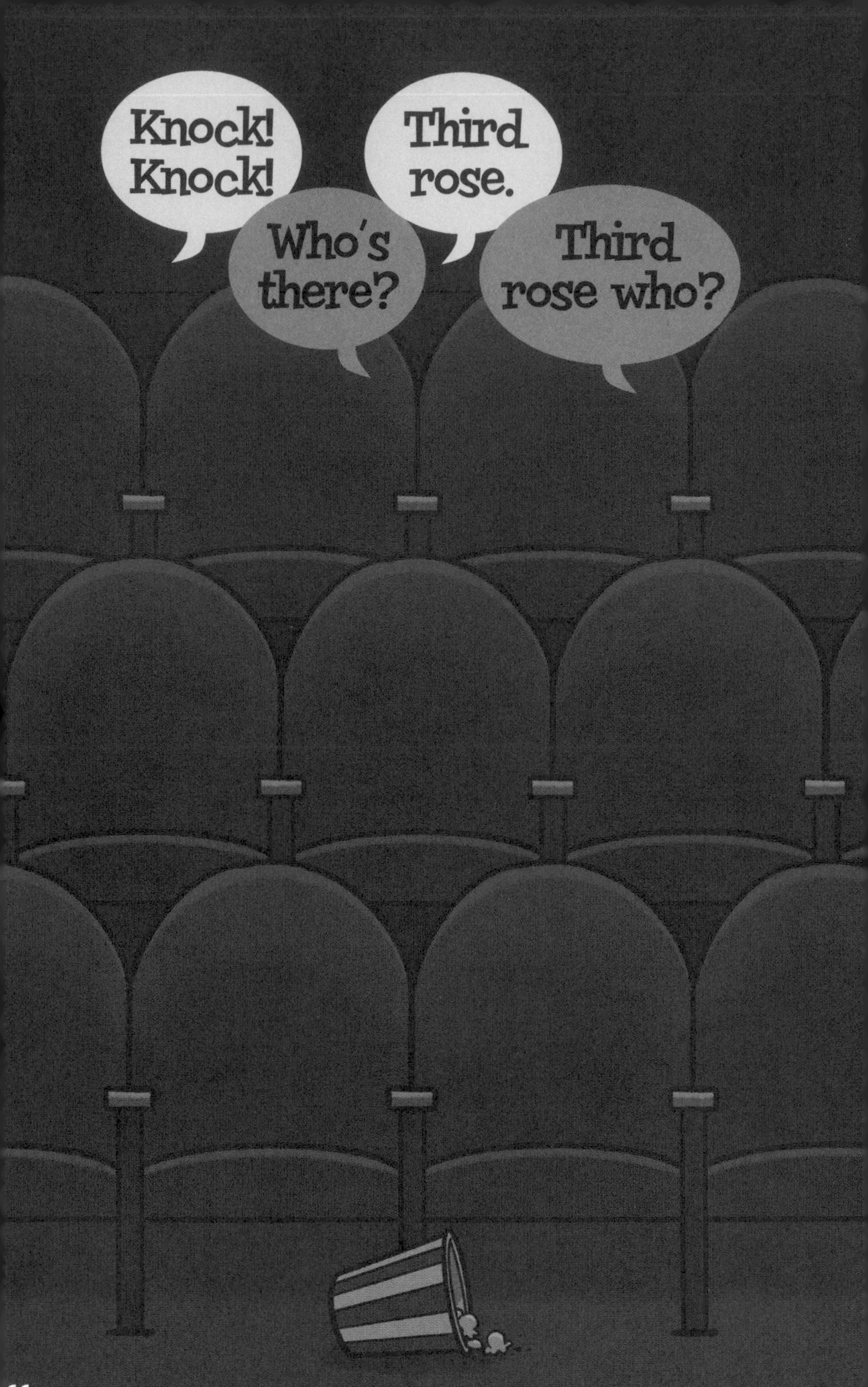
Knock! Knock!
Who's there?
Third rose.
Third rose who?

Third rose located behind the first and second rows in the theater.

Knock! Knock!

Who's there?

Fiddle.

Fiddle who?

Fiddle make you happy, I'll let myself in!

Knock! Knock!

Who's there?

Wendy.

Wendy who?

Wendy door is open I don't need to knock.

Knock! Knock!
Who's there?
Hippo.
Hippo who?
Hippo birthday to you!

Knock! Knock!

Who's there?

Stew.

Stew who?

Stew late for so many questions.

Knock! Knock!

Who's there?

Todd A.

Todd A. who?

Todd A. is your lucky day!

Knock! Knock!
Who's there?
Sadie.
Sadie who?
Sadie magic word and I'll tell you!

Knock! Knock!

Who's there?

Nose.

Nose who?

Nose body knows more jokes than me!

Knock! Knock!

Who's there?

Barbie.

Barbie who?

Barbie Q some burgers this weekend.

Knock! Knock!

Who's there?

Tish.

Tish who?

No, thanks. I brought a handkerchief!

Knock!
Knock!

Who's
there?

Phillip.

Phillip
who?

Phillip
your
water
bottle
before a
long hike.

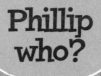

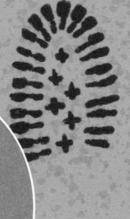

Knock! Knock!

Who's there?

Gino.

Gino who?

Gino me after all this time, don't you?

Knock! Knock!

Who's there?

Ray.

Ray who?

Ray member my name, please!

Knock! Knock!
Who's there?
Zany.
Zany who?
Zany body home?

Knock! Knock!

Who's there?

Toucan.

Toucan who?

Toucan play at that game!

Knock! Knock!

Who's there?

Les.

Les who?

Les share these jokes with friends!

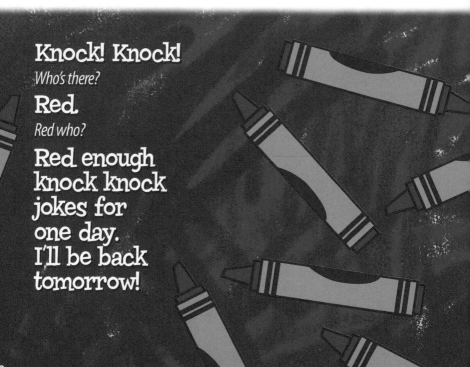

Knock! Knock!
Who's there?
Red.
Red who?
Red enough knock knock jokes for one day. I'll be back tomorrow!

Who made this book?

Super Funny Knock-Knock Jokes and More for Kids was made by the people who bring the weekly *Kid Scoop* page to hundreds of newspapers!

Kid Scoop **believes learning is fun!** Our educational activity pages teach and entertain. Teachers use the page in schools to promote standards-based learning. Parents use the *Kid Scoop* materials to foster academic success, a joy of learning, and family discussions.

Over 25 years of experience in the field has taught us that children learn when they are engaged in the subject. We know that our puzzles and activities draw children into the page. This stimulates children's interest, and they then read the text.

When Fox Chapel Publishing discovered *Kid Scoop*, they knew that there were lots of kids looking for something just like this!

Vicki Whiting – Author

Vicki was a third-grade teacher for many years. Now she loves teaching kids through the weekly entertaining and educational *Kid Scoop* page. People often ask where she gets her ideas for each week's page. Vicki says, "I listen to the questions kids ask. We answer those questions with every *Kid Scoop* page!"

Jeff Schinkel – Illustrator

Jeff has loved to draw his whole life! As a kid, sometimes he was drawing when he should have been listening to the teacher in class. That's when he knew he should go to art school, where he would want to hear everything the teachers had to say! Jeff attended the Academy of Art University in San Francisco and now he loves teaching kids how to draw!

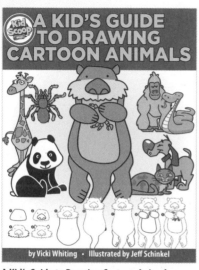